THIS BOOK BELONGS TO:

Printed in the United States of America.
First Edition.

ISBN: 979-8-234-20030-3

WRITTEN BY: Teresa G. Lusk

ILLUSTRATED BY: Ambriel Treviño

CREATIVE DIRECTOR: Daniel Stombaugh

Some ideas are planted long before they are written. I thank God for the creativity at work and for the young girl whose excitement helped bring this story to life. I also dedicate this book to the people closest to me who shared in this vision and offered their support, encouragement, and prayer.

- Teresa G. Lusk

How To Use This Book

This book helps children notice lies in their thoughts and replace them with truth.

Use Anywhere

Home, classroom, counseling, or small groups.

How to Read

Read slowly. Pause after each lie and ask:

- "What is this lie saying?"
- "Have you heard it before?"
- "What would Sweet Little Truth say instead?"

Say the Truth

When Sweet Little Truth speaks, pause and have the child say it out loud. Repeat together if helpful.

Lie #5 (Key Moment)

When the story says the bully brings in lie number five, stop and ask:
"What is that lie for you?"
"What does your bully say in your head?"

Let the child name it. This is the most important part of the book.
Read Again.

Hi friend!

Did you know that sometimes we have what I call The Bully in Your Brain? This little bully visits now and then, trying to tell you lies and make you feel small, scared, or ashamed.

But I have great news for you! I want to introduce you to my friend, Sweet Little Truth, who comes in like the wind to push the lies away.

As you read about the lies in The Bully in Your Brain, some of them may sound familiar to you. That's because we all have similar thoughts from time to time. Come along with me as you read and learn how to build truths that chase the lies away!

—Teresa G. Lusk

Additional Resources
By
Teresa G. Lusk

For Adults

Talk About It: Healing the Trauma Your Past Left Behind

For Children

Other books and titles in this mental health series can be found at www.truestorypublisher.com

True Story
PUBLISHER

Your head is like a house.
So don't let anyone live there,
not even a mouse.

"There's a bully in your brain, you say?"

Well, he doesn't get to stay!

And what does he have to say?

He tells five little lies, but they must go away.

Because Sweet Little Truth sweeps them out of the way.

LIE #1

Lie number one says you'll always be alone,

But every sad day will pass, proving you have won.

LIE #2

Lie number two says, “Eww! Shame on you!”

But Sweet Little Truth says, "Good job — look at you!"

LIE #3

The bully in your brain drags in lie number three, and says, "Look! No one else is like me."

Sweet Little Truth says, "That's his plan, don't you see?"

So repeat, "I'm so special, there's only one like me!"

LIE #4

Then comes lie number four, knocking at the door.

He says, "There's no reason to be happy anymore."

But Sweet Little Truth says, "Chin up, there's joyful feelings to explore."

LIE #5

The bully in your brain tries to bring in lie number five... but this one is yours to find.

Sweet Little Truth steps in, "Not so fast, shame on you!"

We all have a bully that tries to tell us lies.

But do not forget the power of
Sweet Little Truth,
who also lives inside.

OTHER RESOUCES BY TERESA G. LUSK

Talk About It! Healing the Trauma Your Past Left Behind is a lighthearted, approachable guide to understanding and working through trauma in a way that feels safe, clear, and doable.

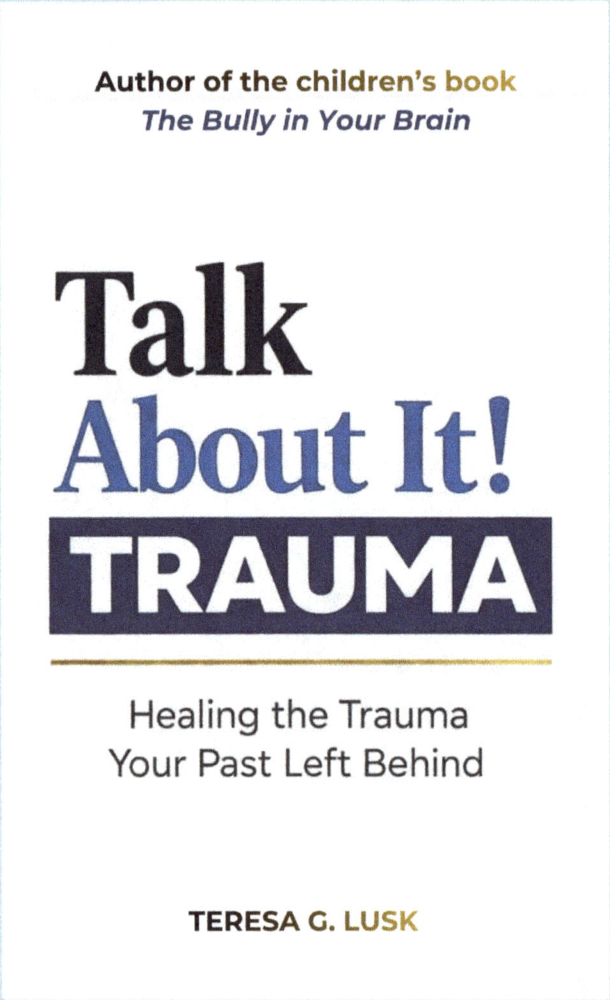

Designed to take the heaviness out of healing, this book helps you explore your story without feeling overwhelmed or stuck in it.

Through simple explanations, guided reflection, and interactive exercises, you'll learn how trauma shapes thoughts and emotions—and how to begin changing those patterns with clarity and compassion.

It invites you to talk, write, and engage with your experience in a way that makes healing feel accessible, not intimidating.

True Story
PUBLISHER

Visit Our Website and Submit a Picture of the Bully in *YOUR* brain!

Discover more books and resources at

www.TrueStoryPublisher.com

About the Author

Teresa G. Lusk

Since 2009, Teresa G. Lusk has been helping people of all ages understand and manage their thoughts, feelings, and emotions through counseling, coaching, and other approaches.

She is passionate about helping children use visuals to notice the bully's lies and respond with truth, and she also offers books and resources for adults to support trauma healing and emotional growth.

This book is part of a growing series of children's mental health stories, covering topics like anger, honesty, and more.

www.ingramcontent.com/pod-product-compliance
Lightning Source LLC
LaVergne TN
LVHW080002210926
848481LV00012B/3652